BURNING HEAVEN

Burning Heaven

Jim Minick

WIND PUBLICATIONS

Burning Heaven. Copyright © 2008 by Jim Minick. Printed in the United States of America. All rights reserved. No part of this book may be reproduced in any manner without permission, except for brief quotations embodied in critical articles or reviews. For information address Wind Publications, 600 Overbrook Dr., Nicholasville KY 40356.

First edition

International Standard Book Number 978-1-893239-81-4
Library of Congress Control Number 2008929155

Acknowledgments —

Front cover photo by Fred First, www.fragmentsfromfloyd.com. Author's photo by Sarah Minick.

Parts of this book first appeared—often in radically different form—in: *ALCA-Lines, Appalachian Heritage, Appalachian Journal, Conservative Review, CrossRoads, The Journal of Kentucky Studies, The New River Free Press, Now and Then Magazine, Pine Mountain Sand & Gravel, Potato Eyes, Red Crow Poetry Journal, Stitches, The Virginia Biological Farmer,* and *Blue Fifth Review Online.* Thanks to the editors of these magazines.

Thanks to Radford University, the Virginia Center for Creative Arts, and Hindman Settlement School for support of this project. Many folks read and commented on various parts of this book. I'd specifically like to thank: Sandra Ballard, The Southern Appalachian Writers Cooperative and Hindman gatherings, Rick Van Noy, Parks Lanier, Dick Hague, Frank X Walker, Michael McFee, Rita Riddle, Theresa Burriss, Barbara Ewell, Hilary Siebert, Grace Edwards, all my teachers over the years including my family. And, of course, the best editor I know, Sarah.

For Sarah,
the poem I kiss every morning.

Contents

Part I *Angels' Voices, Ever Singing*

Dehorning	3
Mountain Laurel	5
Still Born	6
Uncle Bill's Puzzles	7
Gigging	9
After Supper	10
Fullness	11
The Hayfield	12
Angels' Voices, Ever Singing	13

Part II *Trying to Tell Time*

Trying to Tell Time by Splitting Wood	17
Rest	18
Uncle Mark	19
Attic	20
Digging Potatoes	21
Heft	22
The Brier's Last Days	23
A Wash of Brightness	24

Part III *Wings*

Naming the Mourning Dove	27
Walnuts and Worm	28
Crows	29
How Goldfinch Remembers to Fly	30

Glee	31
Wood Duck	32
Flight over Big Branch	33
Wings	34

Part IV *Trespass*

Trespass	37
Dry	38
The Meadow	39
Tuning	40
Even from this Distance	42
Test Run	43
Blackwings	44
Site R	45
Easter Snow	46

Part V *Singing the Pebble*

Sycamore on Big Branch	49
White Oak, Once Forked	50
Ghost Stump, Sun Music	51
The Bear to the Hunter	52
Sestina for Chaucer and Second Period	53
Breathing in Whispers	55
Singing the Pebble	56
Annie	57
Dogs Unstack Wood	59
Takings	60

Part VI *Flicker and Ash*

I Dream a Bean   65
Crossword   66
Gifts   67
Hips   68
Flicker and Ash   69
And Yet We Always Will   70
This Light Beyond   71
Witness   72

About the Author   75

Part I

*Angels' Voices,
Ever Singing*

Dehorning

I shove the kicking calf into the chute.
Uncle locks head between bars.
The others smell the first,
hear its cries, grow more skittish.

Uncle thrusts worm pill
down bawling throat,
plugs in the dehorner.
I pet soft forehead, ask, "Why

we do this?" Uncle waits for the tool
to get white hot, then looks at me.
"We're making these calves into angels.
Don't want them to look like the devil now,

do we?" I shake my head
and watch him work the circle
of heat. He cradles the calf's jaw,
shoves dehorner onto new nub.

And then he waits
through smoke and smell of singed hair,
burning flesh until the nub falls off.
Then Uncle burns the second.

The calf drools, gives up
bucking just to bawl.
"Boy, you ever been butted?"
I nod. "Imagine that cow with horns."

I feel ribs where cow shoved me
into fence, know that horns rip.
Finished, Uncle nods and I open gate.
The calf trots to huddle with the other.

I go back in to fetch another
and spit out the acrid smell
of burning heaven.

Mountain Laurel

White cups touched with pink,
a saucer of pollen for each bee;

A Sunday drive in the mountains,
laurel thickets lining the road;

Grandma hobbled by arthritis
looks to me: "Pick me a laurel."

"You can't," Grandpa complains.
"It's illegal, the state flower."

His words hang between us.
"I know," she replies, then points

and tells me to break and bring her a stem.
I do and resurrect her request

each spring to breathe in this memory,
to hold what no law can touch.

Still Born

From the shadows of dreams,
Uncle Harry wakes me
to a moonless night.

Silent with sleep, we stumble
across the yard, tripping
on lantern circles of light.

In the barn, the cow, white
and black, heaves in the straw—
just two pink hooves protrude.

We kneel to tie twine,
wrap rope around a pole,
grasp and pull together.

Her eyes bulge and watch us,
her breaths are rasps of strain,
of tiredness and terror.

Each pull and heave
burns our palms,
squeezes out knees.

Thighs. Chin. Eyelashes.
To produce a calf
already dead.

Outside in morning light,
the others, shadows
in mist, wait for milking.

Uncle Bill's Puzzles

1.
In his shop, he jigsaws the outline
of Virginia, tiny teeth whirring
through plywood cutting the path of the Potomac,

Byrd's surveyed straight edge, jagged
line of western mountains—the traced triangle
now a silhouette in his hands.

Next the counties fall away, fragments
of a whole state, ninety chips of places
foreign to his lumberyard hands.

With tweezers, he holds each county, paints
a different color, and waits for dryness
to print Floyd, Fluvanna, Caroline.

No need to wrap this Christmas gift
he hands me, his newly-moved nephew.
He waits, then asks, "Where do you live?"

2.
Uncle Bill considers his too-small
basement, and then the empty hayloft
of the barn next door. He wants

some place to hold the whole United States.
He'd have to heat the hayloft, sweep it out,
of course, but he thinks it might do.

He dreams this each evening in his cramped shop,
a work-light islanding a quiet man
and roaring saw. A new puzzle of Maine

nestles Vermont and New Hampshire,
each state, a puzzle itself of counties,
becoming pieces in this country of growing puzzles.

People would come to work their home states,
to hold rough wooden edges of mountain
and river and memory before starting the next piece.

Gigging

"A pitchfork works best," Grandpa explains,
handing me his favorite, smooth handle,
long teeth. "Walk upstream and poke
under roots." He sends me across
the May meadow to Red Creek, gigging
for his frying pan a fish I've never seen.

Wading in, I have to learn to walk,
toeing the rocks, teasing the undercut
to glimpse black flashes from lightning bolt
roots. I throw my fork in mud, bounce it
off slate. Once I fall and laugh in frightened
wetness; black bodies brush my feet.

Soon I slide through current, pitchfork poised.
At a sycamore, the streambed sinks, creates
a pool of hovering fish. I wait for clouds
to break the glare, aim—water dripping—
and throw. The fork cuts water and flesh—
on its teeth, a silver sucker captures the sun.

I spear two more that day, ending the hunt
in scales that weigh in different measure, eyes
that see in different light. I trek back
the plowed fields to Grandpa, his iron skillet,
smell of fried fish, and a mouthful of bones.

After Supper

After supper, Grandpa pouches his lip,
spits clean any strays, and approaches the sink.

In his undershirt, he leans on the counter and begins
this ritual of cleaning sink, drawing water,

and washing dishes. The bowls fill his hands,
shine like whiskered face, find their nested

place. Each glass he inspects with finger soft,
then pauses before picking up the plates.

With soapy hands, drooping belly, this farmer
who cuts quilt patches and cusses every

cow, stomps to the table to lean under,
hawk and spit in his rusty coffee can.

He wipes his chin and belches soft,
then returns to the sink to shimmer in each plate.

Fullness

The oak becomes rib in my hands, the knife
shaping stick into smooth spoke, a whittled
bone to frame a basket for eggs my wife
will weave, her hands pulling tight sinewy strands.

With each stroke, I remember Grandpa's hands
full of days and patches he cut for quilts.
The squares and octagons for Wedding Rings
and Shooting Stars he traced and snipped then pinned
together, awaiting her needle and thread.
When they died, we found ten sacks of patches,
a love no more sent to hands no longer bent.

Again late at night, I think of Grandpa
when the air squeezes my lungs and I try
sleeping in a chair like he did, the phlegm
filling his throat, the ache wracking his ribs.

The Hayfield

In the sweet, heavy smell of alfalfa,
the clickety-clack of hay-rake joggles
the music of memory: in this same tractor,
he once sat in his Granddaddy's lap,
raking the wind on this same unwinding field.
To the rhythm of rake, he hums the one hymn
his dad always whistled with each squeeze
of udder or bellowed with the thunder's roll.
"Then sings my soul," he boomed
over black and white backs, tails slapping,
milker pulsing, his baritone soothing the herd.
The last swath raked, he turns to watch
barn swallows dart like eighth notes
over the field of windrows strung out
in stanza form, awaiting the next refrain.

Angels' Voices, Ever Singing

For Hazel Hensel and Sarah C. Minick

Hazel's voice ratchets like a rusty porch swing;
it bumps against syllables, rasps through ribs
to emerge from her small body beautiful, but rough.
She can't sing except through the piano, her fingers
winging her dreams. Every Sunday after services
and full-spread dinners, Sarah, her sister, joins her
on that bench, Hazel's fingers sounding the chords,
her foot stroking the pedal, Sarah's voice singing
high quavering melodies. They start at the front
of the Methodist hymnal: O For a Thousand Tongues to Sing,
Come, Ye That Love the Lord, their shoulders swaying,
Holy, Holy, Holy, Lord God Almighty,
and Come, Thou Almighty King, until they ring
the final note of Angels' Voices, Ever Singing.

Part II

Trying to Tell Time

Trying to Tell Time
by Splitting Wood

Like the arm of a clock I shock
this round of wood with a heft
and a swing and a blow of the maul

to the face of the cherry chunk.
My hips are the pivot of this timepiece,
minutes measured out in thunks

that echo across the hollow.
The cherry splits into slabs
the color of flesh while sap

seeps to stain the chopping block.
I count the rings, a fingernail
to tick each circle's tock—

109, I think,
but who can count the rotten
heart, the seed's slow start,

the seconds clicking off
the centuries? And where
do you start this numbering

of years, this journey back
to before there were ever
any seeds, any tears?

Rest

In woods beyond fields
they cleared and planted,

we rest in shade.
Each worn tombstone,

a dull, dry tongue,
speaks only to us

who clear away honeysuckle
and mark our spots.

Uncle Mark

Dad, in his Sunday suit, bends
in this ceremony to time, grips
cold handle and silently lifts.
This he has done for his father and mother,
this he now does for Uncle Mark.
The six lean away from the pull of the dead,
swing their free arms for balance.
I follow, knowing soon I will bend,
soon I will be lifted.

Attic

Found in my grandparents' attic:
model railroad—tinsel trailing from the tracks;
porcelain-coated pisspot—bottom rusted through;
shiny, black Sunday shoes—my size;
snakeskins—papery thin—crisscrossing joists;
a globe, the world mapped out, on a broken stand.

Digging Potatoes

We grub for orbs of light: Kennebecs,
Pontiacs, Yukon Golds,
earth eggs perfect in their potatoeness.

We examine each spud predicting futures—
"Home fries," for a warty one,
"A mountain of mashed," for the next.

We work down these rows of dying plants,
work down winter crate by crate,
work down the dusky dark of day.

Heft

For Scott

I should not do this, yet I wash dishes,
take out the trash, make this narrow bed.

He should do it all—feel the hot soapy
slickness of bowl, pick up the heft of waste.

But he dozes in the next room, his breath
far slower than any Coltraine tune.

Before his nap, we talked of Auden,
"About suffering, they were never wrong,"

and Eliot too, though, I did not say
this April had been the cruelest yet—

his voice a slur, his thoughts slipping into
the black hole behind his ear where cancer

eats the bone. It is only a matter
of lost hopes, brief words, few days. He watches

as I make the single bed, new sheets pulled
tight as I tuck in the corners of grief.

Together we stumble the short distance,
then he settles into a long, slow sleep.

Outside the mowing crew tractors along,
sickle bars chattering, cutting the phlox,

wild breath of spring that colored the ditches.

The Brier's Last Days

For Jim Wayne Miller

In his last days, the Brier sleeps in fits,
like an achy child dreaming
of floodwater washing his grandfather away.
He stares past the TV news
and daydreams seasons his memory can hold:

driving the plow behind his mules, the point
whispering into the earth;
a summer porch with grandparents,
the corn all hoed, beans all strung;
a speckled trout, a deep pool and a campfire bright.

Sometimes his memory clouds like a muddy spring,
so he just listens to his breath, each gasp
a snag in his throat like a crosscut saw
on a locust knot. He knows the cancer
grows, an oak gall on his lung.

And he knows these dreams must keep him awake.

A Wash of Brightness

Onionskin yellow,
pokeberry purple,
bloodroot red—
each stain soaks reed
and basket-weaving hands.

Black of oak bark,
walnut shell brown,
marigold orange—
in this miracle of color
we dye in a wash of brightness.

Part III

Wings

Naming the Mourning Dove

For Helen

Helen mourned the truth
I should not have told her.

Like the dove, she sighed
a descending breath of regret.

For her, the dove sang of joy,
a quiet greeting to the morning sun.

Who is to say Helen isn't right,
or that this song could not exact

both the blackness of loss
and the joy of dawn?

Walnuts and Worm

We know the change of seasons by the rain
of walnuts, knocking on our roof, tapping
the shoulder of our dreams. Outside morning
frosts to icy clouds on globes of green,
the yard littered with bushels of fallen earths.

The worm moves slowly inside his little planet,
hungry and shouldering his dream of heaven
where he really does sprout wings.
But first he eats the bitter rind, teeth
tunneling to pile high the yellow
frass of time, and then the burrowing deep.

Crows

On the road ahead black wings flap
like a widow's shawl. I slow to crush
the pain, end what another created.

But I turn into a giddy fool of grief—
the wings are whole, belong to glaring eyes
and claws that shove off toward the leering sun.

When I think of the closeness of death
I remember these mating crows,
the black fire of their joining before

they spring from ashless pavement,
not some mythic phoenix,
but real and angry and alive.

How Goldfinch Remembers to Fly

Does Crow forget his feathers
like we forget our feet?

Like a step, does he just open
and fall, trusting his wings

and the weight of air to hold him aloft?
Goldfinch, though, must know

the weight of doubt, his flight
a fall held back by wings and song.

Crow flies straight and strong.
Goldfinch dips and rises,

a yellow grace note, a golden melody.

Glee

Wrens in rain
love the woodshed.
They dart in the rick
picking spiders
from bark of split oak.

Then they pause in the tin-loud rain
to clatter and rattle their glee.

Wood Duck

When I hear the wing-whistle
of wood duck, my fingers ache.

When drake circles cove, my bones
hollow, the marrow dissolves.

She sings her "weep, weep" to call him
and I watch each follicle darken

to gloss-glitter of sun on feather.
The drake lands to belly-kiss the pond.

She calls again.
I swim to her.

Flight over Big Branch

Circling the sycamore, the red-tail
dances with darters,

shadows swirling in currents,
snails dizzy on spirals.

The hawk kettles a draft,
sifts light with her tail,

winds up the spine
of wind to sail

to the high knoll where
jimson weed blooms white,

pollen drifts in breezes—
tiny meteorites.

Wings

At dusk she waits in the meadow
for veined wings and tiny bodies
falling through this startling heaven.

If the bats fly off too soon, she stares at trees,
bare branches a maze of filaments, a sky
full of veins that lifts her fluttering into the night.

She knows heaven then
doesn't float far away but sits
cupped in the thin lines of each hand.

Part IV

Trespass

Trespass

I shoot the earth,
the bullet furrowing frozen crust,
shoulder still jarred by expected blow.

Half-deaf, glare-blind, I shoot the night,
the barrel flames out,
stars chitter in cold laughter.

But at least I don't shoot the coon hunters
slipping down the hollow,
baying dogs in tow.

Their flashlights reveal
their path as I watch
in the scope.

Dry

Headlights narrow the night.
I drive, John holds Lulu his favorite Chihuahua
stiff and panting despite winter air.

Frantic beyond worry, my elderly neighbor
paced all evening to call, finally, for help.
"She keeps giving but she just can't.

Her pups have sucked her dry."
Each teat swollen, each eye wide as the vet's
yawn who mentions spaying, fills her with shots,

bills us and keeps her the night.
John does not have money to spay all his dogs.
But he owns a pistol.

He asks me to carry the box,
wait, and then dig the grave. The blind pups
mew when I pick them up.

They crawl and search for milk.
I do not touch soft fur, sharp teeth,
anything but this den turned coffin.

Outside, John cocks the gun,
rests barrel on each head, looks away, squeezes
his eyes shut. Four times,

the flare lights his face.
The blasts numb my ears even after
I empty the box, cover the hole,

stumble the dark path home, the dirt still under my nails.

The Meadow

From the shade of this giant hickory,
paths once spread through the meadow like roots
tendriling and bare. I called the cows
then from this tree, whistling
to wait for lumbering ladies who hungered
for corn, udders swaying, calves trailing.

Years later, no more paths spread
like capillaries from this hickory,
no cattle trample dusty lane,
no boy runs through grass chasing
calves, chopping thistle. Instead

fluorescent flags, hidden by knee-deep
grass, mark boundaries for lots,
paved paths, a cul-de-sac.

Tuning

We huddle behind bleachers
and wait in scrambled shadows
of stadium lights, stiff wool
of uniform scratching necks,
fingers freezing to brass,
the scoreboard timer
too slow and too fast.

The drummers practice a soft patter
on each other's helmets.
Sweely fingers her solo,
sucks her mouthpiece to keep it warm.
I mark time and walk the lines
tuning the band with Kim, first clarinet.
She plays C, holds it long
while each player replies,
one by one, and like I know
I say sharp or flat or OK,
then move on to flutes, trombones,
all the winds—

not thinking about my mace,
that stick I have to throw
at the brass's *crescendo*,
that twirling giant toothpick
I never catch and always hope
doesn't spear a majorette—

not thinking about Cooper,
my predecessor, who last year
on Star-Spangled Banner

started one side of the band
two beats ahead of the other,
cracked us all in that frying pan
of a football field while the town
sang and laughed at the same time—

and Cooper trying to yell away
everyone's humiliation,
to halt our cacophonous
implosion, to stop even this
memory of tuning and grief,
the timer still ticking
too slow and too fast.

Even from this Distance

That night, we made love on the ribbed back
of a '67 Chevy pickup.
The hardbed of our childhood cracked
with each stroke as we tenderly cupped
Eden. Before, we used to skip
stones on the Conodoguinet, wade till we shivered,
pass notes in Spanish, miss church to dip
skinny and naked in the stream that mirrored
your arcing body. Later, you shunned
Newburg for Long Island, then Madrid,
dealing for IBM, cocktails, promotions.
I work for a dream of a farm seeded
in Virginia. Yet even from this distance,
you send more than a card at Christmas.

Test Run

From four hundred miles   away they fly
faster than their own   thoughts, their own
sound, that slurred   symphonic tympani.

Doomed destiny: Claytor Lake Dam.

They approach with practiced   perfection, pointing
their noses, nefarious   knockers of the world,
into the wall   which can never wail for mercy.
At one thousand feet,   they thank the Lord and
push their buttons   pretending the battle real,
the blast erasing the   image their eyes still see.

Test run done,   they turn majestically
over my broccoli   and beans, brushing
the pods with their wings.   With practiced patience,
I hoe, just like   Julio in El Salvador,
just like Vo-Dinh   in Viet Nam.

Blackwings

On the Viet Nam War Memorial

Blackwings and a parachute
  on green shoulders
    uniformly swing into transport plane.
                              Nobody knows
      Blackwings of empty-bellied bombers
      circle like tsetse flies back to base.
                            the trouble
      Black as boots, hand grenades,
      body bags, labeled and stacked.
                            I've seen
        Blackwings in snow,
        outspread to fly home
                        Nobody
          unable to enfold
          mourning mothers
          disillusioned sons.
                      but me
          (Mice-gnawed bones become
          granite-chiseled letters.)
                    Nobody
            Blackwings,
          an open grave,
            corpseless
              only images:
              ourselves and
                but me
          John Calvin Smith
                but me
         David William Hensel
                but me
         Marvin Melton Burns

Site R

> *Site R is a mountain ninety miles
> from Washington, D.C., under which
> government officials plan to escape
> in the event of nuclear war.*

When I beat my thumb on your side
like testing a melon, you thump

hollow, ripe for "War," whispers
sentries' sunglasses; "Winter

of all winters," whistles tires
whirring into tunnels, gates

closing behind. Mangled mountain
trapped by military miles

of barbed wire fence, once you played
with bison, threw winters

at Iroquois, taught them how to
survive. Now uniformed souls burrow

into your cored heart, build
a city in your granite belly.

Hollow hill, barrow of us all,
home of the free moles who dig deep,

when will you crumble?

Easter Snow

Pink blossoms of peach, blueberry's fragrant hanging cup,
an orchard of apples and pears all rimed this morning

to frozen stillness. Elm's mint-colored leaves,
yellowbells and daffodils covering the woods

now all white, all gone. What in me has already died?
A bum knee, a hollow tooth, a belief in resurrection?

No, I still believe in the miracle of spring,
even on this white-whittled day, even in this world

falling apart. Just not the Jesus story,
the human separateness. We will rise

like everything else—in the mouths of maggots,
the purple of asters, the feathers of vultures.

But there will be no more flowers this year.

Part V

Singing the Pebble

Sycamore on Big Branch

Each veined leaf, ridged and valleyed,
is a map of the face of the sun.

Each plate of bark seizes that slippery
sun and turns it into rainbow-drops of sap.

At the base, the corky trunk hollows
to beetle tunnels, ant caves, coon dens.

We sit on the sycamore's knee,
a living bench covered by nutshells,

a century's gathering of squirrels.
Under us, the tree's roots explode,

a fireworks booming slow. In the tips
high above, star-fragments birth

to pollen, flicker in the sun and drift away.

White Oak, Once Forked

The leftover hurl of hurricane
rives it open, this wooden wishbone,
giant slingshot, tuning fork

for the wind, now only half
of any of that. How old,
who knows, centuries at least

but no rings to count, its heart
composted to duff, bedding for bears
in a barrel-den trunk—

no more,

the lid blown open, marrow sucked dry.
Instead of black bear's long dream
and sigh, this trunk fills white with snow.

How will the wind ever sing again?

Ghost Stump, Sun Music

A stump is the ghost of tree,
empty shoe of one long leg
that danced to any waltz of wind.

But this spider has spun a ghost
of a ghost, a dew-covered web
flat and even atop fleabane.

The orb weaver's slip of silk
circles all of what once was
the hard surface of an old stump,

each strand a ring, a year this ghost
dancer traced overnight.
Or is this spider a musician?

The dead-level web becomes
a record, LP of invisible
tunes, strands circling, spider

a diamond needle that splinters
shining light, releases it
to smooth grooves, the sun's own music.

The Bear to the Hunter

How long have I run from you, Orion?
I'd say before north was even north,
the moon only a stone. Yet you keep
your sword always drawn, old friend,
just in case this pattern of dots releases us.

You and I, we ride this sky of myth
and memory: that time you lost your way
in the black night's forest, it was my tail
and me pointed you home; and when I gnawed
the same bone in that long, lone blizzard,
you killed a deer, tender the knife—did you know
I watched you then drag it to my den?

Sestina for Chaucer and Second Period

Before the morning bell, I must erase
yesterday and write new lessons in stone.
Words of dust, white on black, these notes
lead through crowded hallways to letters
of chuckling Chaucer—he who rooted
our jokes, our warts, and our wordy power.

The bell wakes me to the power
that strolls into the room. Sleep erased
incompletely from their eyes, they take root
in stiff seats, daring me to stone
them with cheerfulness or more letters
in Chaucer's foreign tongue. I note

their bleary minds, they note
my concrete smile, (the power
of Chaucer must live), together we letter
our day with new meaning from the unerase-
able past. First the miller's stone
thumb of gold, furnace for a mouth, root

wart of a nose, flush and root
into the corners of their mouths. I note
smiles, snorts even, and write in stone,
"Never underestimate the power
of a thumb." The miller's life partly erased,
enter the wife of Bath and her lusty letters

to five dead husbands. Still she love-letters
her gap-toothed way to men as she digs roots
for another potion. We cannot erase

her altar door. Next the high, sweet notes
of the Pardoner's offertory overpower
the miserly, convinces even the stone-

faced pinchfists to give their gold stones
for relics of pig's bones, pillowcases lettered
as Our Lady's veil. His sonorous power
is our power abandoned, uprooted
for the moment. For the moment, all these notes,
love letters, jokes can be erased

like dust on black stone. But the tendriling roots
of letters split stone. The bell rings notes
of power: our time, but not Chaucer, erased.

Breathing in Whispers

In the great open spaces of my lungs,
prairie grass bends and breathes in whispers.

In the knobby frame of my body, red oaks
split boulders, lean into buds.

In the mad trickle of my veins, the Atlantic
rolls in sleep, its waves the color of starfish.

In the black holes of my eyes, stars flare,
Venus shakes, the Milky Way disappears.

Singing the Pebble

At river's edge, he found
all water, earth and mirrored sky
in one small stone, hazel and round.

He rolled it on his tongue,
tasted springhead and creek,
the roiling river, the sky's lung.

He carried it between lip and gum
the rest of his life, trying
to sing this one pebble unsung.

Annie

She pounces and paws the earth,
the collie madly focused on nothing

I can see, her black-and-white body
crouched to play. When I move,

she yips and circles, ears forward,
eyes bullets of attention. An attack

again—on dirt? What pulls her so?
What causes this panting frolic?

And then I eye the game—my shadow!
Annie is chasing the almost-me,

the untouchable border
my body creates.

I sway and dance and laugh
with this dog, her scurry and bark

so intensely joyous, so consuming.
Surely she knows she'll never catch

this dark prey, this headless snake
of an arm I waggle between us.

And in her scrambling, she too
creates a ghost, an echo

chasing her chasing me.
When clouds hide our shadows,

Annie waits, tail rigid,
mouth ready to swallow

what disappears every night
when the earth wobbles

and we all dance and play
with our own laughing shadows.

Dogs Unstack Wood

after mouse again, or bunny,
or even last week, groundhog
(that didn't escape like others),
something weary of fangs and blood.

Becca the lab climbs up top,
wobbling once on falling wood,
ears forward, legs crouched,
six feet high and hoping to pounce.

Jake the shepherd bites hickory
and oak, whole-body yanks
what I so carefully ricked,
a ton of hours he unworks

with snuffle and snort and heave,
blind on scent, fresh heat,
the firewood already kindling
spark of mouse darting deep.

Takings

Like coyote and coon,
crow and neighbor's dogs,

like mouse and hawk and fox
and legions of buzzards,

buzzards blackening air,
like all of these, I too

return to this carcass
of buck somehow dead

by this spring it went to
to ride that trickle back

into the ground.

Yet in two days the body
is resurrected with

claw and beak, tooth and saw—
eye sockets emptied,

neck muscle slicked clean,
even lips nibbled bare,

the bones a twisted helix
like broken DNA.

I want the antlers, their
hardness for knife handles,

their perfect arcs punctuated by tines.

Breath renders clouds of fog,
left arm bears down on tip,

right works saw—back/forth back/
forth—whispers blade's fine teeth

in the frost-covered morn
bone dust falling on boots.

Part VI

Flicker and Ash

I Dream a Bean

sprouts from my hand,
its roots trace lifeline

then plunges into vein,
a tendril filling

every capillary.
From each finger,

a leaf, broad and green.
From the loveline,

the first bloom.

Crossword

When Byrd and Hallie fought, did Byrd walk out,
shove through the gate to tramp this pasture road
like I do now, head down, arms
stiff, fists tight? In the rainy dusk,
did he pound this hill, trip on ruts and shout
at leafless oaks—rain slipping down
the leathered nape of his neck?

Around this bend, deer snorts forced
his thoughts to fly with four white tails,
leap on leap to some more ordered field.
And at this end where lane meets woods and fence,
darkness found him pissing out his anger.

Byrd had to turn, then, to face
the rain and Hallie. He looked away from wind-
blown water and saw scattered rocks
where once his parents' chimney stood. But he knew
that uphill, planted in a row, his walnuts
marked off his gaiting step.

By the barn, he saw one light inside
and Hallie concentrating on her crossword.
Peep frogs in the pond and the rain's tin
song told him to go dry off.

Gifts

For Sarah

She gives, he takes. He gives, they take,
not her. The couple's lives wanting
wholeness, a circle they can trace.

She gives love, bread, hugs,
and supper every night at 6:00.
He takes it all and gives quizzes,
meetings, classes, and millions of comments
on millions of papers. They take it all,
want more, lick him dry
like cats licking the milk bowl,
leaving him smooth and hollow inside.

He doesn't like it, wants to give her
more than a paycheck and two hugs
to frame her day, wants to complete
the circle. But he doesn't know how,

except maybe for this.

Hips

All day I look at hips,
rolling swales of marbled mountains,
sleek slopes of burnished hills,
landscapes I cannot visit,
nor want to.

But at night, I am home
in the smooth curve of your roundness,
hollows and scented crevices,
tender peaks I touch with lips,
tasting the sweetness of that hidden spring,
familiar yet always unknown.

Flicker and Ash

That moment the Tree of Life ignites in us
fingertip branches flicker and the sacred trunk flares up;
that moment when all seeds spark, each a lick of sun
scattering on new ground; in that moment
the hardwood density of life consumes itself
then floats away as ash.

And Yet We Always Will

We sleep in the same bed
under the same quilt,
the same roof,
the same arch of milky stars.

Yet we dream apart,
buried in separate forests
of that other world.

Death too has this loneliness.

No matter how we drift off—
holding hands, hugging,
even one inside the other,

we cannot go on together.

This Light Beyond

There is a light beyond this light,
a radiance you never see
that presses in, that holds in place,
that stops the shatter of every
bulb in every Milky Way—
a gentle touch of what?, this light.

Until one night you watch your hand
reach through this other light,
like putting on a coat, knuckles
traveling through a tunnel of brightness,
a coat of light you wear
without ever knowing,
and your hand *feels* light,
like it has no bones, knows
no gravity, just this momentary
wonder as it finds its way to the bedside lamp,
and before that hand, those fingers touch
the switch, you see it, just now
this other light, this light beyond,
this light of everything, even the night.

Witness

For Kevin and Melissa

What if at dusk we stretch out on our backs to watch
the last bat slip through winter's grip
with copper-colored back and wings dancing like falling leaves?

Or if we wait all day by the spring-cold pond
for fleecy wood ducks to fall from nest,
first-swim to mother waiting in cattails?

What if we feel called to search for the peeper
and his peep, never seeing gold-ringed eyes,
only tracing the bubbled throat, the shrill call of love?

What if we did nothing all day and all night
but witness this world's steady unfolding?

We too would bloom like the serviceberry
delicate and white.

Jim Minick is the author of two books of poetry, *Burning Heaven* and *Her Secret Song*. Also he has written a collection of essays, *Finding a Clear Path,* and edited *All There Is to Keep* by Rita Riddle. Minick has won awards from the Appalachian Writers Association, *Appalachian Heritage, Now and Then Magazine* and Radford University, where he teaches writing and literature. He's garnered grants from the Virginia Commission for the Arts, the Virginia Foundation for the Humanities, and a residency at the Virginia Center for the Creative Arts. Minick's work has appeared in many publications including *Shenandoah, Orion, San Francisco Chronicle, Encyclopedia of Appalachia, Conversations with Wendell Berry, The Sun, Appalachian Journal, Bay Journal News,* and *Wind,* and he writes a monthly column for *The Roanoke Times New River Current.* He lives, hikes and gardens in the mountains of Virginia with his wife and three dogs.

Printed in the United States
125141LV00003B/48/P